Evan's World

Evan Apseloff

Ryan Apseloff & Stanford Apseloff

OHIO DISTINCTIVE PUBLISHING
Columbus, Ohio

Artwork by Evan Apseloff. Elephant art by Ryan Apseloff. Story by Stanford Apseloff.

© 2022 Evan Michael Stanford Apseloff, Ryan Arthur Apseloff, and Stanford Apseloff. All rights reserved.

ISBN 978-1-936772-29-2
Library of Congress Control Number: 2022906547

For Mom, who is always outnumbered.

Hi. I'm Evan, and I'm eleven years old. I have a little brother, Ryan, who's eight years old. Actually I'm eleven and a half, and Ryan just turned eight. We like Oreos, gaga ball, LEGOs and Harry Potter. And art.

I like to draw and paint when nobody's telling me what to do. But Dad always wants me to draw animals—not my favorite.

One day I watched a BrainPop video on Cubism. It's art with boxy shapes and lines. I liked it and thought I could do something sort of like that. So I did.

I asked Dad if I could draw his portrait, and he told me to draw myself instead. "A portrait says more about the artist than the guy in the picture," he said. "Draw yourself and that won't matter."

So here I am, wearing my favorite Spiderman Halloween shirt.

Note #1—I'm not smiling all the time, and I actually have five fingers on each hand.

Note #2—Except for things like actual number of fingers, everything in this book is totally true, especially the stuff about Ryan.

Self Portrait—pencil on paper

Painting—pencil on paper

Sometimes I paint, but it's hard to erase—especially watercolors. So things don't always turn out the way I like. This painting in my drawing was actually in color, but for this book it has to be black and white.

Ryan likes to paint, and he's really good, but he makes even more of a mess than I do. One time at school he spilled an entire bucket of purple paint water onto the floor. The teacher had to use a huge sponge to wipe it up. She never did get it out of the cracks.

Lobby—pencil on paper

Before I learned to draw or paint, I learned how to spell. The first word I learned was "LOBBY." It was the big button in the elevator. We were on vacation, and we kept going up and down because we would forget stuff in the room.

Ryan wasn't there. He wasn't born yet. He missed some fun times.

Breakfast—pencil on paper

Our day starts with Mom making breakfast. I'm easy—I like cornflakes. Ryan usually wants a hardboiled egg. I told him that eggs come out of a chicken's butt. He doesn't believe me.

We both drink milk. One time Ryan spilled a whole gallon. That's why the cat hangs out at the table.

Gardening—pencil on paper

Mom does lots of other stuff too—like gardening. That makes everybody happy—the rabbits eat her flowers, the deer eat the blueberries, birds eat the strawberries, and caterpillars eat the tomatoes. And mystery animals come in the night and eat whatever's left. Except the cucumbers—Mom makes spicy pickles out of those.

Sometimes Ryan helps with the gardening. He likes to use the hose, but he always ends up really, really wet.

Hockey—pencil on paper

One time I told Mom I wanted to play hockey. She said you have to know how to skate. So I asked her to take me skating. Who knew it could be so hard? They gave me this walker thing, like for an old person, and told me to push it around on the ice. So I'm thinking how can I hold a hockey stick and do this at the same time—impossible.

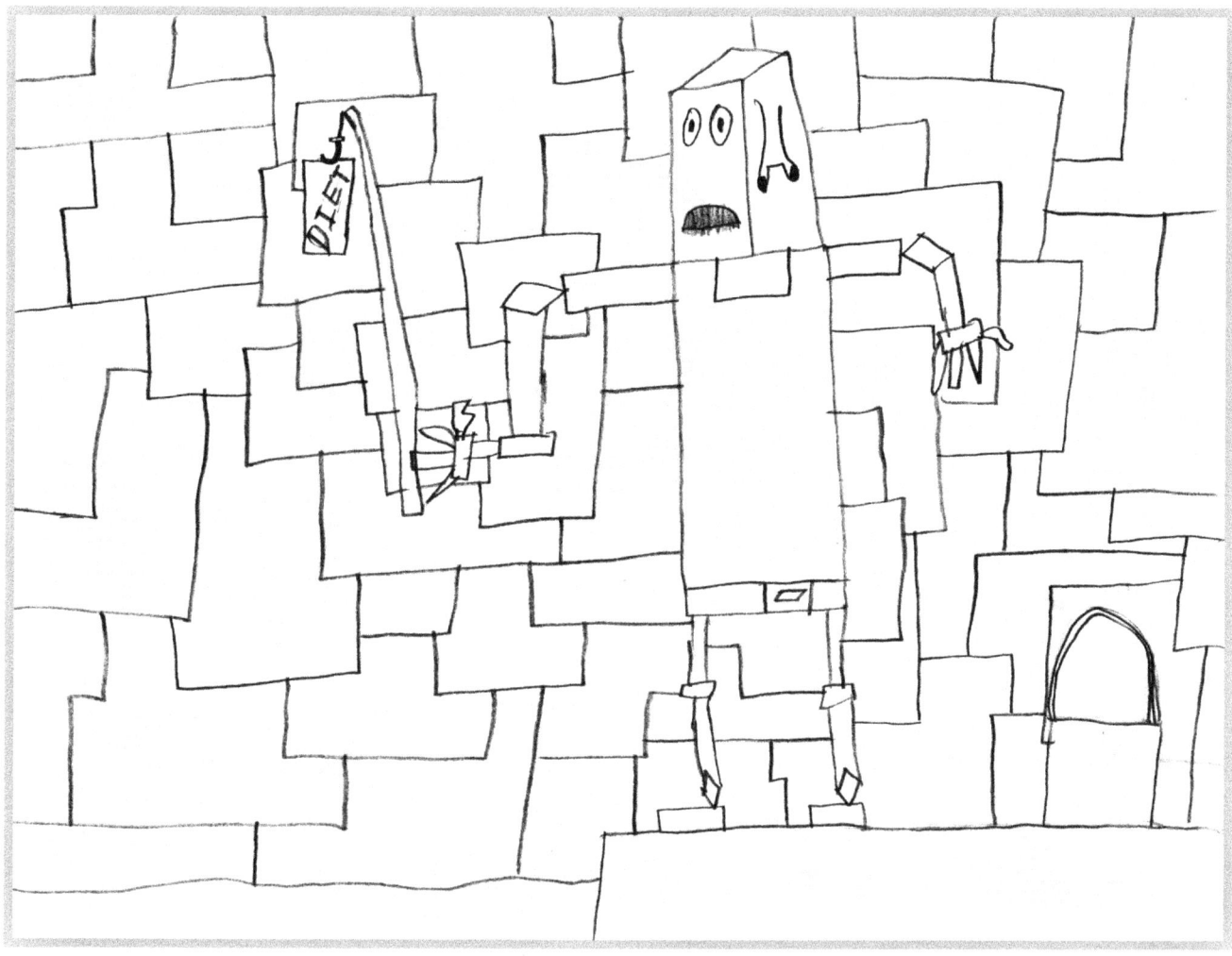

Fishing—pencil on paper

Sometimes we have fish for dinner. Mom likes the white ones. Dad likes salmon. Ryan likes ones without bones.

Dad says if you want to catch fish, you have to use the right bait and know where to go. He said most fish are caught from boats, which makes sense because why would a fish want to come where there's land?

Some fish are probably smarter than we think. I wonder if maybe they're playing tricks on us when we end up catching junk.

Magic Trick—pencil on paper

Did I mention that Ryan and I like magic? Dad taught us how to read minds and we learned some tricks from watching YouTube videos. We wanted to pull a rabbit out of a hat, but I think we don't have the right kind of hat. We also don't have a rabbit, and our cat's ears are too short.

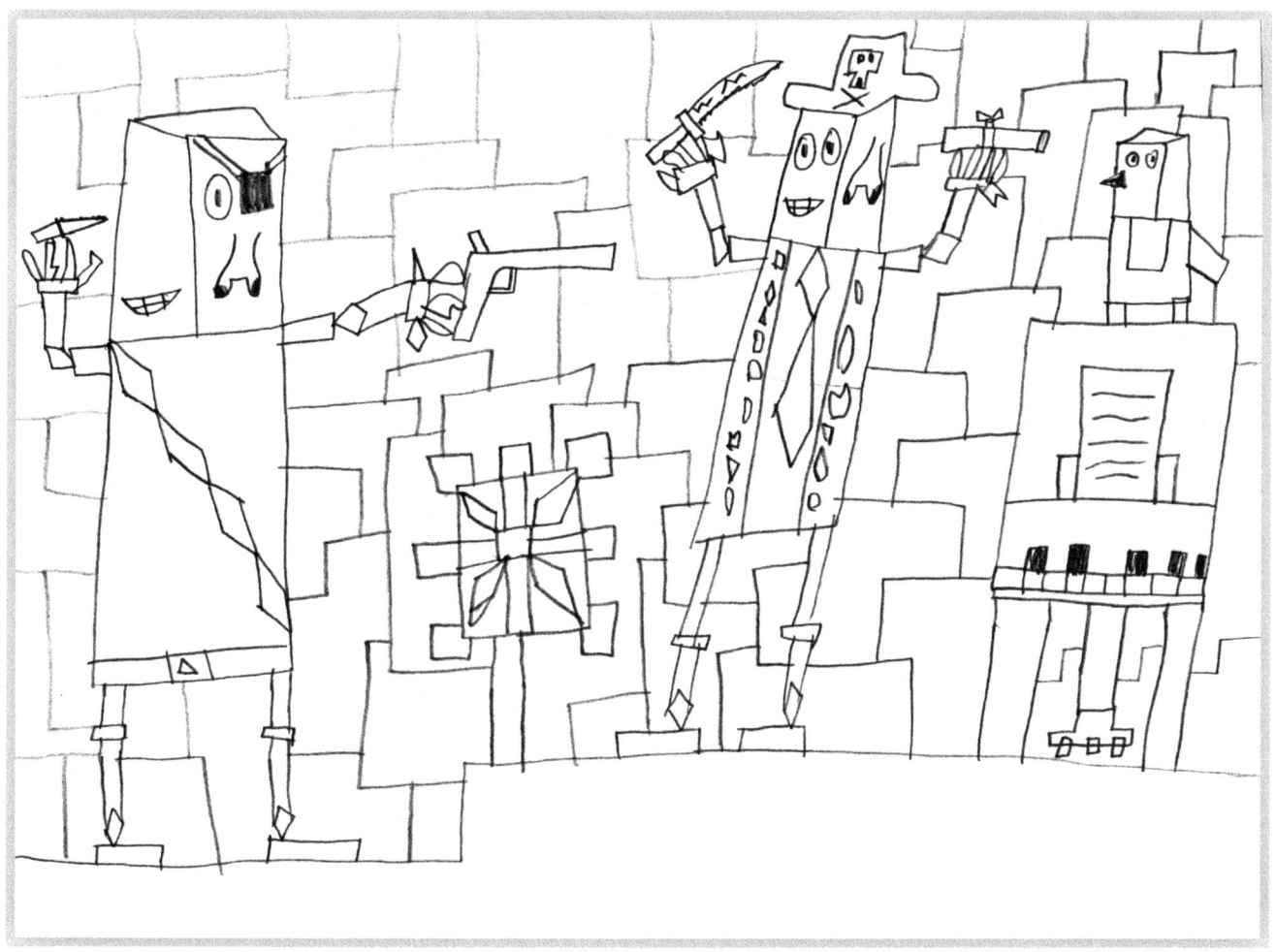

Pirates—pencil on paper

Ryan and I like to play pirates. We built a ship with cardboard boxes in our playroom. The only thing that's missing is a parrot. That and real weapons. But we're good at pretending.

The piano is what Dad calls "symbolism." It's because I like the music for *Pirates of the Caribbean*.

Chess—pencil on paper

Ryan and I like to play chess, but we both hate to lose. We're not very good, and sometimes we change the rules. Also Ryan got an all-white chess set for Christmas because he wanted to paint half the pieces to look like bear fur. He hasn't done that yet, so playing is a challenge.

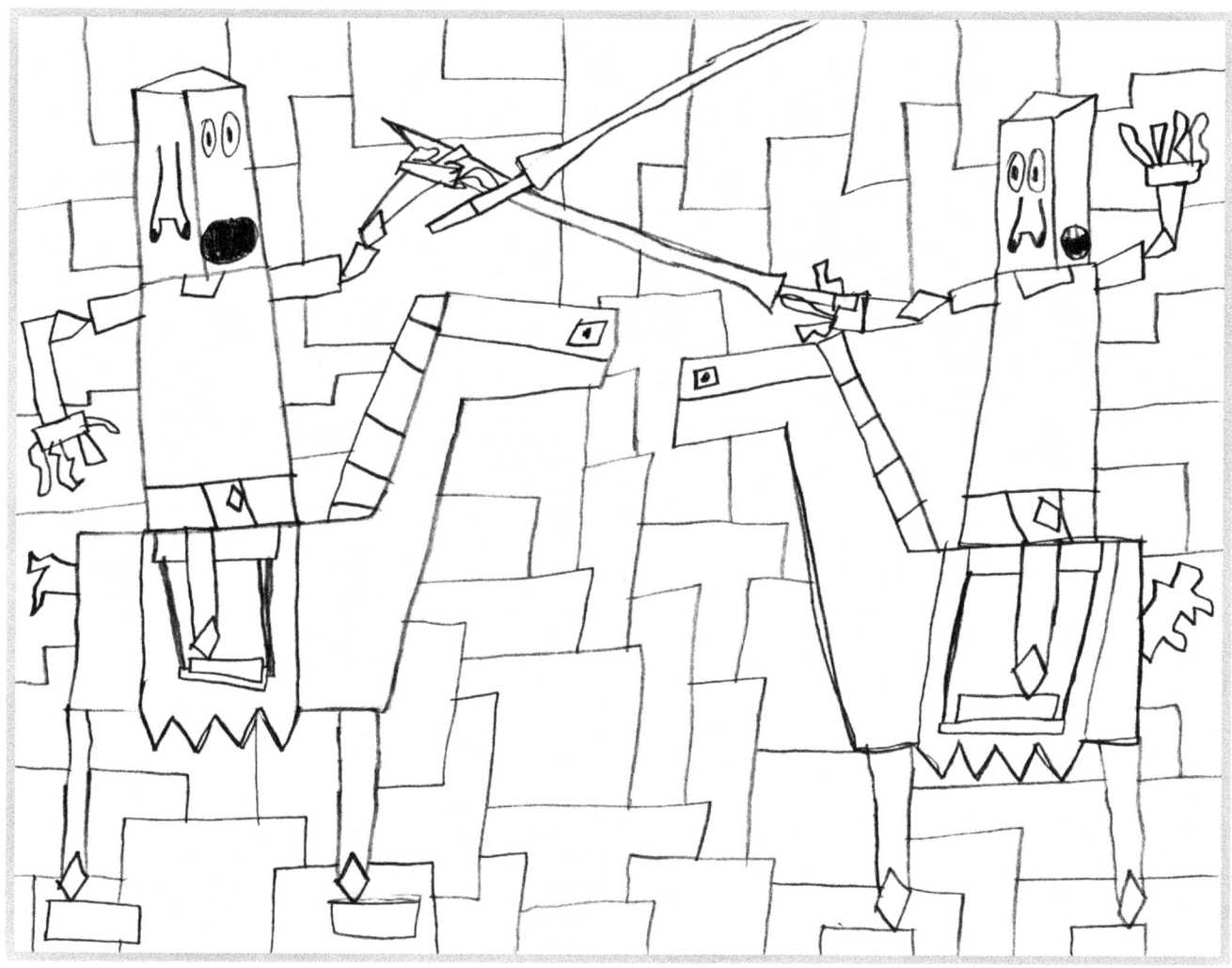

Combat—pencil on paper

Sometimes I fight with Ryan. Not like this, but it still hurts. The knights on horses I saw at a jousting tournament at the Ohio State Fairgrounds. It looked pretty dangerous. I'm not sure why my parents wanted me to see that.

Someday I want to ride a horse. I know Ryan will want to race—he's super competitive.

Badminton—acrylic on canvas

In gym class at school we played badminton. Dad says there's supposed to be a net, but the teacher didn't tell us that. Besides, it's hard enough without something getting in the way. On the other hand, maybe if we had a net, I wouldn't have a bruise on my shoulder.

Fortunately badminton rackets are light. Tennis rackets are like caveman clubs. With tennis you need a net to keep it from being dangerous.

Tennis—pencil on paper

I tried playing tennis, but it wasn't much fun. You have to come really close to get the ball over the net, and then if someone hits it back, it's going way over your head.

When Ryan and I played tennis, bees were flying in and out of the post that holds the net. Ryan started swinging at them with his racket. That was a couple years ago, before he knew that bees sting. He doesn't like tennis anymore.

Bowling—acrylic on canvas

I think bowling would be fun. I've never been to a real bowling alley, but Ryan helped me set up the next best thing in our playroom. We used cardboard bricks for pins and a small playground ball for the bowling ball. Ryan wanted to poke holes in it, but I told him that would be a bad idea.

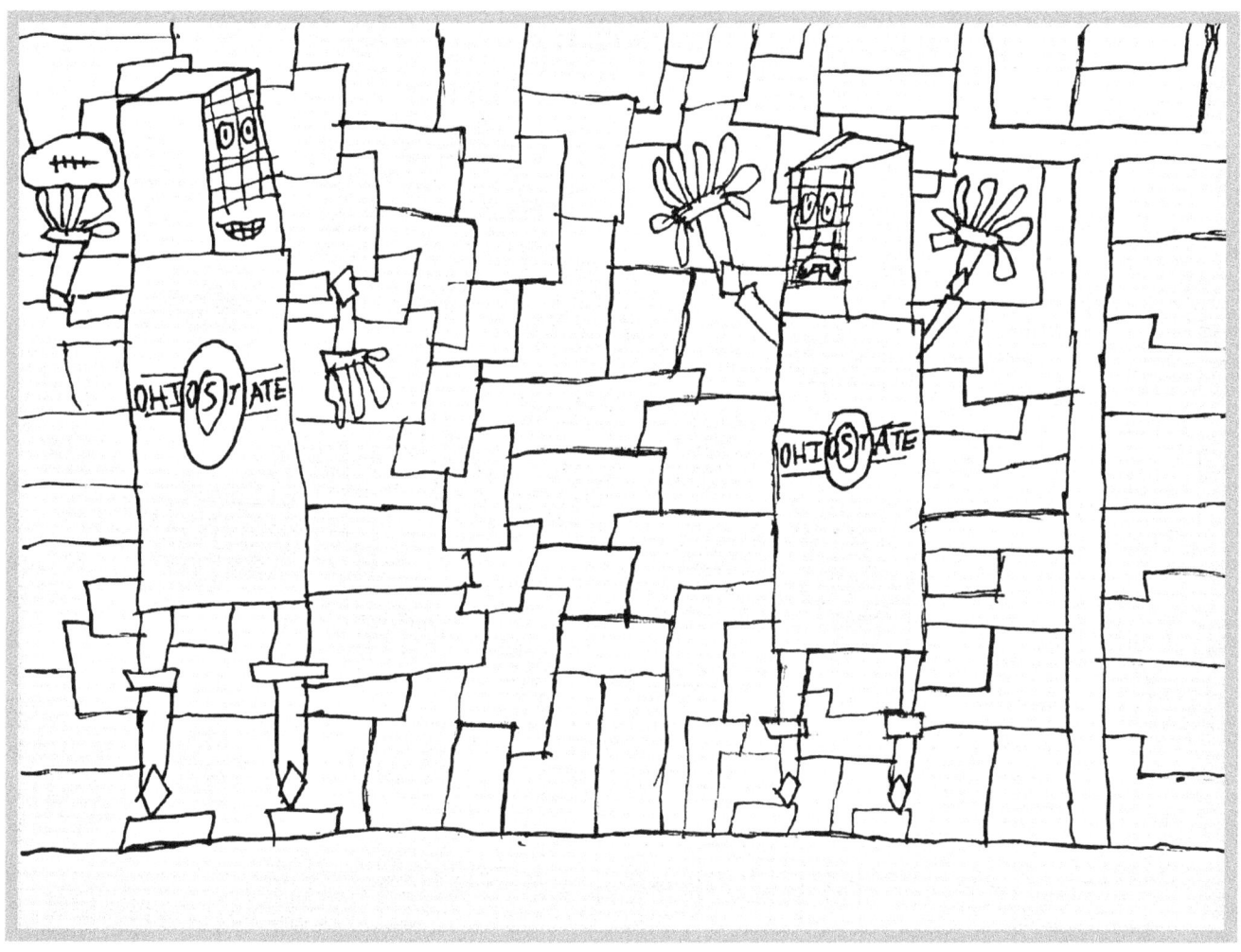

Football—acrylic on canvas

Dad likes to watch football, as long as his team wins. I think that's because his dad always rooted for the Cleveland Browns. So now Dad watches the Ohio State games, and usually that puts him in a happy mood.

Mom and Dad tell me that I used to watch with them when I was really little. They say that one of the first words I learned was "Touchdown!"

Poker—pencil on paper

Ryan and I like playing cards. I asked Dad, "What's your favorite card game?" He said, "Bridge." I asked him to teach me, but he said you need four people, and they all need to know how to play. So he taught me poker instead. We didn't play for money, but Dad says a lot of people do.

Please Play—pencil on paper

Dad does lots of work at home on a computer. We interrupt him all the time. Sometimes he stops working and plays with us—cards or whatever. Sometimes he say, "Go draw an animal."

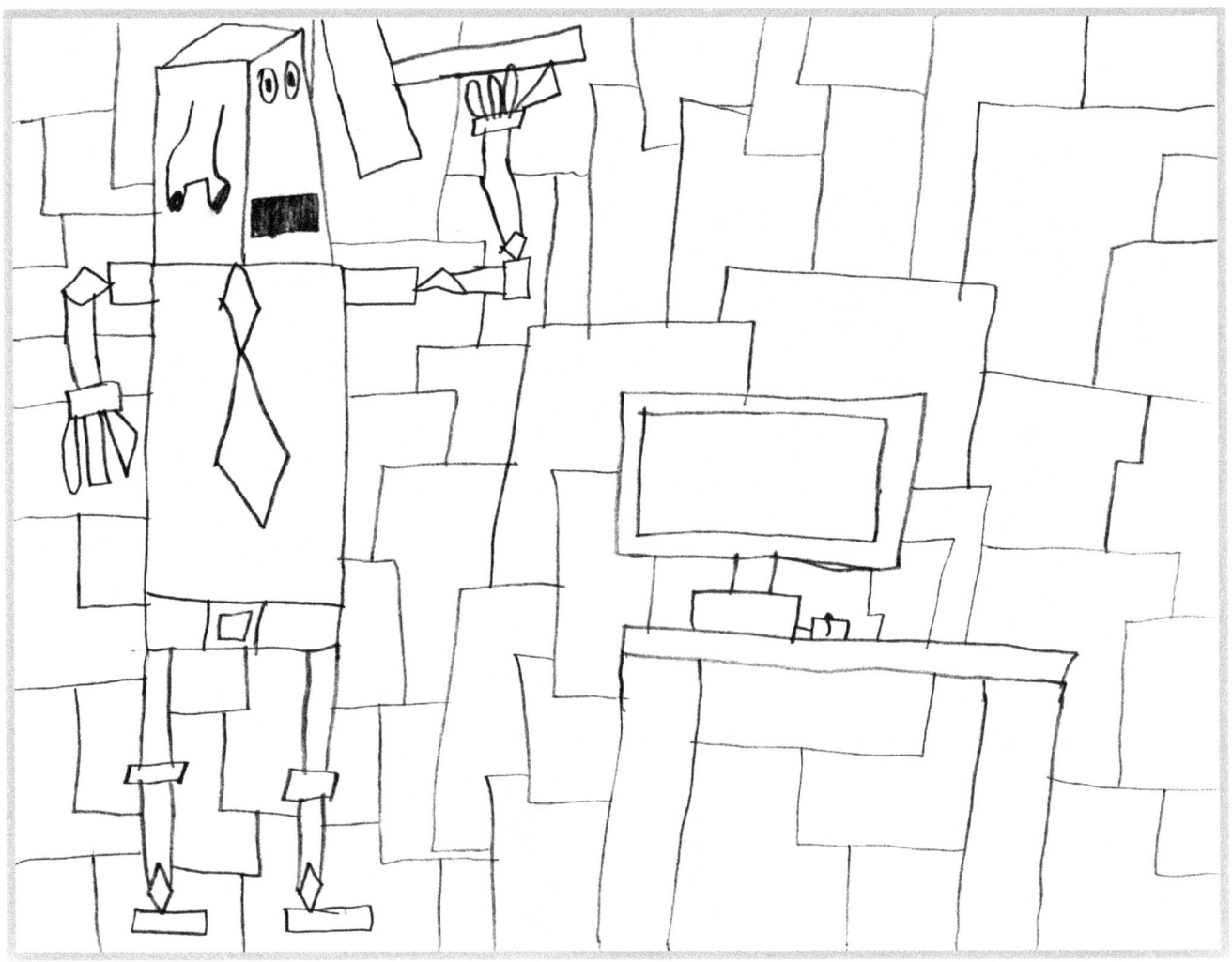

Bad Day—pencil on paper

If you use a computer, sometimes you want to do this. Like when you're about to get a high score and the computer freezes, or you've made a really cool game on Scratch and POOF—it's gone!

Dad doesn't let me use a hammer for anything. He's afraid I'll hit my hand. But as you can see, there's no problem if you just keep your other hand off the keyboard.

Dad won't let me use nails either—you know, for hanging stuff on the wall. I think he's afraid they'll end up on the floor and ruin the vacuum. We already ruined one vacuum with LEGOs.

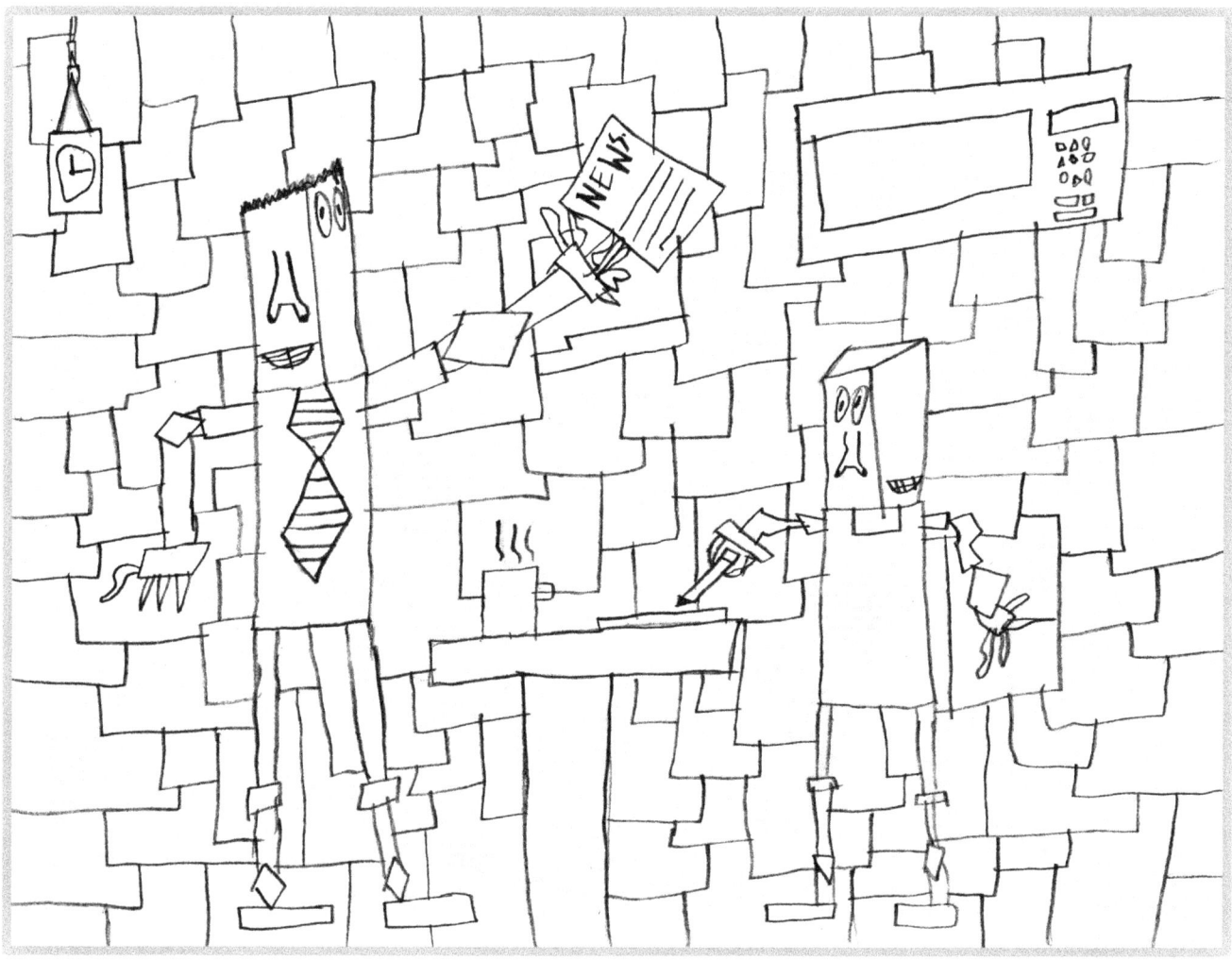

The Office—pencil on paper

This is what I imagine an office is like. Dad says this looks more like a break room. But doesn't everyone drink coffee at the office, and probably they get lots of news, and have a microwave to pop popcorn. And look, somebody is working., writing stuff. Of course there's a clock so everyone will know when they can quit and go home.

I think going to an office will be kind of cool, especially if someone pays me to be there. I have a tie I can wear. It's a clip on so I don't have to worry about it not fitting when my neck gets bigger.

Since this is a pretend office, I put my brother in it with me. I'm the boss, and Ryan's drawing an animal—that's his "work" for the day. He has to finish by 5 o'clock.

Sick—pencil on paper

Sometimes I get sick and have to stay home from school. It's really boring, especially if you don't like drawing animals.

Mom makes me homemade chicken soup with carrots, cabbage, and little green stuff floating on top. I'm usually better in a day or two.

When Ryan gets sick, sometimes he gets really sick. Once he got a ride to the hospital in a fire truck. We didn't have a fire, but still it was one of those red trucks, only there was no ladder on top.

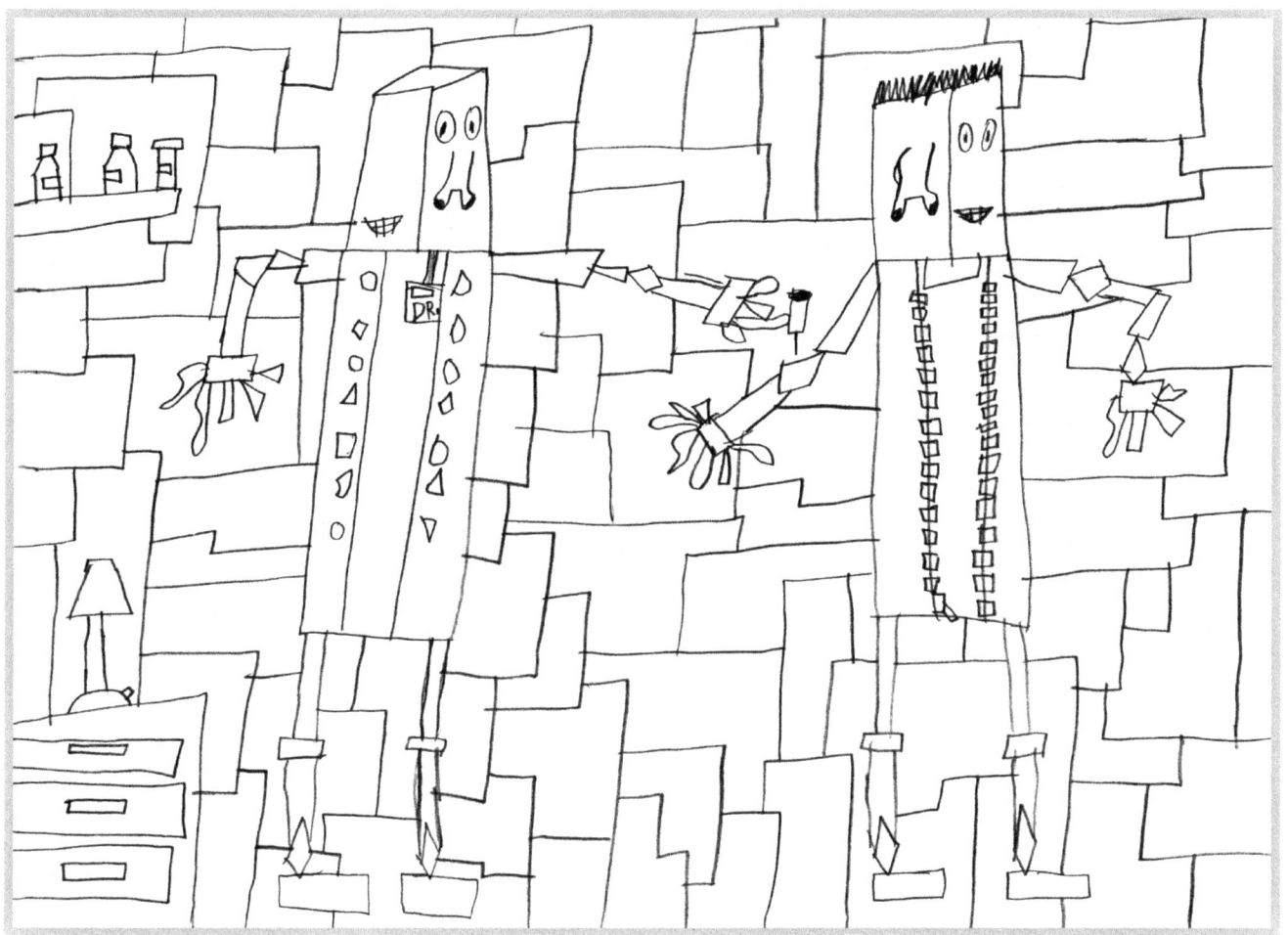

The Shot—pencil on paper

This year for the first time, I got a shot at the pharmacy instead of the doctor's office. It hurt just as much.

The Dentist—pencil on paper

Dentist chair—over there,
Have a seat, if you dare.

I feel like a fish that got too close to the boat! And to make matters worse, I have one tooth growing in on top of another—the dentist is delighted.

Ryan has perfect teeth—almost. One time he dived off the living room sofa onto the coffee table and lost half of his front tooth. The Tooth Fairy didn't give him anything for that—doesn't seem fair.

The last time I lost a tooth, Ryan sneaked into my room late at night and put extra money under my pillow.

Pool—pencil on paper

Dad has two brothers. Uncle Roy is older, and Uncle Glen is Dad's twin. So sometimes we visit Uncle Glen and Aunt Lucia. They have a pool table. They don't let anybody put drinks on it, but I'm doing it here anyway. They also don't have a dart board, but I think that would be cool. Dad says Uncle Glen used to play a lot of pool, but now I think the only one who uses that table is their cat. I should have drawn a cat.

Checker Tournament—pencil on paper

Uncle Glen played in a checker tournament when he was a boy, and he won a trophy.

Dad taught me how to play, but I like chess better—the pieces look a lot more interesting. I've seen lots of checker sets, and all the pieces are always round—why is that? It's not like manhole covers that have to be round so they don't fall into the hole. Checkers should be shaped like stop signs. That makes sense because every time you move a piece you have to stop and wait.

Deadlift—pencil on paper

Uncle Roy is a powerlifter. Most of the time he gets world records, but not always.

He can lift 600 pounds. That's like ten Ryans, but it's only eight Evans.

Turing Tumbler—pencil on paper

Our next-door neighbor Fran told us about this Turing Tumbler game. It's like the opposite of pinball. You put in flippers wherever you want and watch the little balls fall down to the bottom. The good thing about it is you don't need any quarters.

We like Fran. She has friendly dogs and friendly grandkids. Ryan wants to buy her house when he's older so that he can live next door.

On Top of the World—pencil on paper

So that's my world. Dad says it will get more interesting, but I don't see how.

And about those animals that Dad wants me to draw . . .

Ryan's Elephants—pencil on paper

Ryan draws them instead!